Little Pebble™

Fire Safety

by Sarah L. Schuette

Consultant: Shonette Doggett, coalition coordinator
Safe Kids Greater East Metro/St. Croix Valley
St. Paul, Minnesota

PEBBLE
a capstone imprint

Little Pebble is published by Pebble
1710 Roe Crest Drive
North Mankato, Minnesota 56003
www.mycapstone.com

Library of Congress Cataloging-in-Publication Data
Names: Schuette, Sarah L., 1976– author.
Title: Fire safety / by Sarah L. Schuette.
Description: North Mankato, Minnesota : An imprint of Pebble, [2020] |Series: Little Pebble. Staying safe! | Audience: Age 6–8. | Audience: K to Grade 3. | Includes bibliographical references and index.Identifiers: LCCN 2018052293| ISBN 9781977108678 (hardcover) | ISBN 9781977110275 (paperback) | ISBN 9781977108753 (ebook pdf) Subjects: LCSH: Fire prevention—Juvenile literature. | Fires—Safety measures—Juvenile literature. Classification: LCC TH9148 .S376 2020 | DDC 613.6—dc23
LC record available at https://lccn.loc.gov/2018052293

Editorial Credits
Erika L. Shores, editor; Heidi Thompson, designer; Morgan Walters, media researcher; Marcy Morin, scheduler; Tori Abraham, production specialist

Photo Credits
All photos by Capstone Studio/Karon Dubke

All internet sites appearing in back matter were available and accurate when this book was sent to press.

The author dedicates this book in memory of her firefighter friend, Orangy, of Henderson, Minnesota.

Printed in the United States   5866

Table of Contents

Be Safe

You can be safe

if there is a fire.

Plan Ahead

Bo's family has a plan.

They pick a safe place to meet.

Bo makes a map.

Bo looks in each room.

He finds two ways out.

Bo sleeps with
his door shut.
It helps keep out smoke.

Fire Drill

The family has a drill.

Beep! Beep!

It's the smoke alarm.

Get low!

Bo crawls.

He knows to get

under smoke.

Get outside! Bo goes
to the safe place.
He knows not to go
back inside.

Bo knows how

to call 911.

He knows his address.

What to Do

Test your smoke alarms.

Make a plan.

Practice it every year.

Glossary

address—the number and street name of your home

drill—to teach someone how to do something by having the person do it over and over again

map—a drawing or picture that tells you where to go

plan—to decide how something should be done; a safety plan is important

practice—to repeat something over and over so you learn it well

Read More

Cavell-Clarke, Steffi. *Staying Safe.* Our Values. New York: Crabtree, 2018.

Ghigna, Charles. *Dial 911!* Fire Safety. North Mankato, MN: Cantata Learning, 2018.

Honders, Christine. *Why Should I Listen to Firefighters?* New York: PowerKids Press, 2019.

Internet Sites

Fire Safe Kids
www.firesafekids.org/safety.html

National Fire Protection Association: Sparky
www.sparky.org/

Critical Thinking Questions

1. Why should you sleep with your bedroom door closed?

2. Describe how to practice a fire drill.

3. How often should you practice your plan in case of a fire?

Index